FRANCIS POUL~~ENC~~

Suite for Piano

1. Presto
2. Andante
3. Vif

CHESTER MUSIC

(A division of Music Sales Ltd.)
8/9 Frith Street, London W1V 5TZ

Triangle Pianos
SOUTHAMPTON
023 8055 2656

5·95

A Ricardo Viñes

SUITE POUR PIANO

I. Presto

FRANCIS POULENC (1920)

sans ralentir

II. Andante

III. Vif

SELECTED CHAMBER WORKS
from
CHESTER MUSIC

ABRAHAMSEN
Walden Wind Quintet No 2
Preludes 1 - 10 (String Quartet No 1)

N. V. BENZON
Mosaique Musicale Op 54
for flute, violin, cello and piano

BERGE
Yang Guan for wind quintet

BERKELEY
Diversions for oboe, clarinet, bassoon, horn, piano,
violin, viola and cello
Sextet for clarinet, horn and string quartet
Trio for violin, horn and piano
Quintet for oboe, clarinet, bassoon, horn and piano
Concertino for recorder (flute), violin, viola and
harpsichord (piano)

BROWN
Trio for flute, bassoon and piano

BURGON
Four Guitars

FALLA
Psyche for soprano, flute, harp, violin, viola and cello

GUDMUNDSEN-HOLMGREEN
Terrace for wind quintet

HOLMBOE
String Quartets Nos 1 - 15

LUTOSLAWSKI
Dance Preludes (1959) for flute, oboe, clarinet,
bassoon, horn and string quartet
String Quartet
Mini Overture for brass quintet

MAW
Chamber Music for oboe, clarinet, bassoon, horn
and piano

MACONCHY
String Quartets Nos 10 - 13

MAXWELL DAVIES
Anakreontika for mezzo soprano, alto flute, cello,
harpsichord and percussion
Runes from a Holy Island for alto flute, clarinet,
viola, cello, celeste and percussion
Tenebrae Super Gesualdo for mezzo soprano, alto
flute, bass clarinet, harpsichord/celeste/harmonium,
guitar, percussion, viola and cello
Brass Quintet

MUSGRAVE
Impromptu No 1 for flute and oboe
Impromptu No 2 for flute, oboe and clarinet

NØRGÅRD
Spell for clarinet, cello and piano

PAYNE
Paraphrases and Cadenzas for clarinet, viola and
piano

POULENC
Sextet for wind quintet and piano
Sonata for clarinet and bassoon
Sonata for two clarinets
Trio for oboe, bassoon and piano

SAXTON
Echoes of the Glass Bead Game
for wind quintet

SEIBER
Serenade for two clarinets, two bassoons and two
horns

STRAVINSKY
Berceuses du Chat for voice and three clarinets (or
voice and piano
Four Songs for voice, flute, viola and harp
Suite from The Soldier's Tale for clarinet, violin
and piano

WILLIAMS
Japanese Fragments for soprano, viola and guitar

WOOD
String Quartets Nos 2 & 3
Four Logue Songs for contralto, clarinet, violin
and cello

CHESTER MUSIC
(A division of Music Sales Ltd.)
8/9 Frith Street, London W1V 5TZ